Dear Future 9th Grader

Dear Future 9th Grader

The High School Survival Guide for
Academic, Social, and Personal Success

Arielle Morris

Vista Hill Press
A Division of Five Minute Network, LLC
Los Angeles

DEAR FUTURE 9TH GRADER:

The High School Survival Guide for Academic, Social, and Personal Success

Copyright © 2019 by Arielle Morris
Published by
Vista Hill Press
A Division of Five Minute Network, LLC
907 Westwood Blvd., Suite 405
Los Angeles, CA 90024

First Edition: 2019

Cover design by Bojan Rekovic
Logo design by Arielle Morris

Library of Congress Cataloging-in-Publication Data is available
ISBN-13: 978-0-9968377-2-9
ISBN-13: 978-0-9968377-3-6

For Camp Kesem—for showing me that great things can come from terrible circumstances.

Table of Contents

Introduction

Dear Future Ninth Grader,

Hello. My name is Arielle Morris and I am a senior in high school. I was born in Dallas, Texas, and moved to California when I was 6 years old where I have lived ever since.

I was inspired to write this book because I have no older siblings so I had to figure out high school for myself. Makes no sense? Let me explain. I'm writing this book for all the eldest siblings who have no idea what to do once they get to high school. Basically, I am going to be your surrogate big sister who teaches you how to survive high school.

First, a little about me. During my sophomore year in high school, I took a total of 7 classes: AP Psychology, English 10 Honors, Precalculus Honors, French 2, French 3, Biology, and AP European History. Junior year, I took AP Statistics, AP Computer Science Principles, IB English Language & Literature, IB French B, IB History of the Americas, IB Psychology 1, and IB Theory of Knowledge. It sounds like a lot of work, and it was. My GPA is currently 4.67 and that took a lot of hard work to accomplish.

Besides academics, I am in four clubs at school (I founded or co-founded two of them) and until very recently was on an elite club soccer team and my high school soccer team.

It might seem like I have high school all figured out, but I don't. I don't think anyone really does, but I can try to guide you through high school as best I can based on what I have learned so far.

3

So, did you just finish eighth grade? Congratulations, you survived middle school. Or, maybe you are in the middle of the summer before freshman year. Enjoy your freedom while it lasts. It's possible you are reading this book the week before high school starts. Whatever your circumstance, I can help you out. I know high school may seem like the four most daunting years of your life, and in a way, they are. High school is a period of your life when you will feel like you are in a constant state of limbo. You are still young enough to live at home and be treated like a child, but you are old enough that whatever you do will impact the rest of your life. It's kind of scary that teenagers are forced to make decisions that will decide the direction of their adult life, for better or worse. However, high school doesn't have to be as intimidating as it is made out to be in movies and TV shows. With my help, you will hopefully be able to more easily navigate high school. With that goal in mind, I've come up with twenty tips that I wish someone had shared with me four years ago.

Here goes …

Tip #1:

Don't Worry So Much About Your First Day

I remember my first day of freshman year. When I got there, I quickly realized that my orientation tour didn't help me at all to know where anything was. I couldn't find my friends for a few minutes and I didn't want to look like the stereotypical scared freshman that I know I looked like. You remember back in eighth grade, there were those little sixth graders who didn't know where they were going or what to do? Freshmen in high school are the equivalent of sixth graders in middle school. Yeah, it sucks, especially since you were the oldest in your school only a few months ago. This feeling of being a fish out of water will only last a couple of days and after that you'll see that the sophomores, juniors, and seniors are actually pretty nice, except for a couple of jerks. While you'll meet jerks at every school, you might even end up being close friends with some of the nicer upperclassmen.

After you find your friends, decide where to meet during breaks and lunch. I've noticed that a lot of people drop their middle school friends when they get to high school, and that's completely the wrong approach. You might add a couple of new friends to the group, but, it's smart to build upon your core of good friends or join another group of quality kids from middle school whom you also know well.

When you and your friends decide where to meet during lunch on the first day of school, don't pick a table until lunch. Just decide where to meet. Hopefully, you located your classes at orientation so you know where to go. If not, try your best to find your first period class. Usually, teachers are pretty good about being understanding on the first day when freshmen can't find their class.

Once you get to class (hopefully on time, but if not, it's not the end of the world), you need to focus on making a good first impression. Before you even get to school, try your best to be prepared for class. This means to have at minimum a spiral notebook for each class, red and black pens, pencils, an eraser, a binder, and the assigned books for each class. Leave the books you don't need for that period in your locker, but don't expect to always have time to go back to your locker between periods. For math, English, history, and science, usually it's best to bring a three-subject spiral, but don't write on the cover yet. For electives, PE, or a foreign language, bring a one-subject spiral. If the teacher has a list of supplies, get as many on the list as you can before school starts. You probably don't really need to bring a stapler, even if the supply lists says you need one, as you can usually just borrow one from a classmate or the teacher. Once you are in class, sit in your assigned seat, if there are assigned seats, and be respectful. Not all of your teachers will like you and that's life, but you will increase your odds if you do your best to pay attention and show respect at all times. Teachers are much more likely to want to help you if they see that you're attentive and respectful. I'm sure you know what it's like to have a bad relationship with a teacher and you know that never goes well. First impressions are when teachers decide if they like a student or not and it's much better to be one of the students whom the teacher likes.

Expect real homework on the first day, not just having your parents sign something and you're done. It sucks. Up until high school, the first day of school was just social and you got to come home and proudly announce to your parents that they have homework, not you. Sorry, but those days are now over. In high school, expect some kind of review assignment on the first day if there wasn't already summer homework. This is especially the case in math. If you have a class where you don't get any real homework, you're lucky, but don't count on it.

When there is a break between classes, meet up with your friends where you already decided to meet. If you are new to this school system, meaning you didn't go to any of the middle schools that feed into your high school, try to talk to the kids in your classes who seem nice. It might take a couple of days, but be patient and you will most likely find a good group of friends. If possible, try to find friends who share your interests; I promise someone will.

When lunchtime comes, meet up with your friends, but wait to sit down until after the sophomores, juniors, and seniors pick their tables. Humans are creatures of habit. They prefer to sit at the same table as the previous year or years. The unspoken rule of high school is that freshmen take the tables left vacant by the seniors who graduated the year before. Don't steal someone else's table. They will not like it. If you ignore my advice and steal an upperclassmen table, until they graduate they will think of you and your friends as the "morons" who stole their table. The table you choose the first day will become your table and you will probably eat there until senior year, unless someone steals it. If someone steals your table after you and your friends have established it, you will quickly learn how annoying it is.

The first day of high school typically goes by pretty fast. All I remember is a blur of being lost, teachers' syllabi, and lots of names that took a couple of weeks to remember. After you make it past the highly anticipated first day, it will get increasingly easier. It will eventually seem just as boring as middle school, except with a lot more work and stress thrown in as you try to figure out what you want to do with the rest of your life; but high school isn't all that bad. It may seem scary, and I remember how scary it felt to me, but it's not that bad. You will make friends whom you will one day find on whatever social media platform replaces Facebook and you will remember their names, and smile. You will be instantly reminded of the four years that dictated the direction of the rest of your life. Just remember, the first day may seem like such a huge milestone, but in reality, it is just another school day, not unlike any you had in middle school. Just remember to be nice to people and try to make friends who can make school bearable and try to make a good impression on your teachers. See? Easy.

Tip #2:
Take The Classes That Are Right For You

*A*t the end of eighth grade, you most likely met with your high school counselor to help choose your classes for freshman year. Not every student will take the absolute hardest classes offered for their grade. It's just impossible. They are called honors and advanced placement (AP) classes because they are challenging and difficult classes. When deciding on your classes, make an honest assessment of your abilities. If you were in Honors Science in eighth grade and got a C, maybe it would be better to take regular Science freshman year and challenge yourself in a different course. These regular classes are called "CP" in my school system. If you don't already know this, CP stands for "College Prep" and those are the classes that aren't as challenging as Honors and AP, but will still qualify you to apply to four-year colleges. Maybe you are great in a certain subject so you feel you truly belong in Honors. Just make sure that you don't overestimate (or underestimate) which level of classes you should take. Your goal is to put yourself in classes where you can succeed, but also feel a bit challenged.

Don't get me wrong, I definitely think it is great to challenge yourself, but don't feel compelled to challenge yourself in every class you take, especially if you aren't really good at a subject. Try to take one "reach" class a year and the majority of your other classes should be classes that challenge you, but you think you can do well in them. You should avoid taking a class that is so easy that it's boring because no easy "A" is worth it. You should also not put yourself in a class that is so hard that, no matter how hard you study, you can't get the grade you want.

If you really believe the absolute hardest classes your school offers are the ones in which you belong, then congratulations, you are a genius. Good for you. You can probably stop reading my book now. However, if after freshman year you find you didn't get the grades you wanted, take a step back and self-assess. Maybe you shouldn't be taking the advanced math course you planned on taking next year. It's not the end of the world. Remember that when applying for college, your transcript is very important and although colleges want to see challenging courses, they also want to see good grades. If you can't earn good grades in the hardest classes, then consider taking at least one lower level class. It is not a punishment or embarrassment to take a lower level class if you feel it is the right place for you. In no way does taking an easier class mean you are any less intelligent or talented. Find the classes where you can excel and still be challenged and focus on those.

If you have some idea of what you want to do in the future, try to see if your school offers an elective that gives you the opportunity to try it out and sample that field. If you are interested in video production, acting, photography, or some other type of art, find out if your school allows students to try it out. If you are interested in being pre-med, being a psychology major, working in a lab, or pursuing some other type of scientific profession, see what courses your school offers so you can try it out. Whatever your interest may be, check and see if your school has an elective in that area. For example, before high school I thought I wanted to go into video production, so I took the elective my school offered in that subject and hated it. Although it was a pretty boring and unsatisfying class (one of the more difficult A's I earned because it's hard to stay interested when you don't like the subject), it's better to find out you really don't like something in high school rather than in college, when you are paying for your education.

Especially freshman year, take a variety of classes to see what you enjoy. Freshman year is the year before your grades really start to count. Colleges don't take freshman grades into account as much as sophomore and junior year grades. They do count, but not as much. Take the cooking class you really want and maybe skip the Honors math course you think will be insanely difficult for you. Remember, you are at school to learn. If a class is so hard that you won't be able to do well no matter how hard you try, you probably won't learn much of the material as you are just struggling to keep your head above water and, in addition, you also won't be able to focus on and learn the material in your other classes.

If you sign up for a course and after a few classes, you realize you are already miles behind your classmates in your overall understanding of the material, drop it. It is not humiliating to drop a class. In a way, you are doing yourself a favor. By dropping the class, you are avoiding late, frustrating nights of not understanding the material you are going to be tested on the next day. You are not signing up for eight hours of homework a night because it takes you twice as long as your classmates to complete an assignment because you genuinely don't understand it. You are not signing up for a year of stress, trying to excel in a class that is impossible for you. You are not doing yourself any favors blindly "believing in yourself." Instead, drop the class, and replace it with a class in which you have interest and where you will have a chance to do well.

Alternately, if you realize after a few days that the class is so easy you could sleep through it and do really well, drop it. Take the next class up. Again, you are not doing yourself any favors taking the easy "A." You are at school to learn, so learn. Take a class that is challenging and takes some level of effort. If CP math is so easy for you that you could sleep in class and get an "A," you will most likely be able to do well in Honors math and you will actually learn something. You want to find the right balance between being challenged and being able to do well in the class.

Tip #3:
Work on Time Management

*H*ere's the definition of the worst nightmare of a high school student. It's 10:30 at night and you haven't started any of your homework because you wanted to finish season 10 of your favorite Netflix series. You check your phone and see a text from a friend asking if you've finished the huge project assigned weeks ago. The reality is that you haven't even started it yet.

At this moment you realize you are going to be up until at least 2 a.m. and you probably won't finish all your work and if you do, it won't be done well. You've discovered the dangers of procrastination. Now, you need to either pull an all-nighter and do good work, not do it at all and suffer the consequences, which I don't recommend, or do it all really fast.

First of all, why would you do this to yourself? Was that TV show really worth it? You could have spent your time over the past few weeks doing a little bit of work every night and finished the project early. Second, now that you've gotten yourself in this situation, you'd better get yourself out of it. Luckily for you, I'm here to share my years of experience in this exact situation to guide you out of it. Did I say years of experience? I meant to say, I did this once and learned from my mistake.

First, plan out your project so it will be completed before the due date. Basically, create a game plan that, even half asleep, you can use to get the project done to the best of your ability. Do you want "half-asleep you" to make any important decisions? The correct answer is no. So, create the game plan for the project, but don't start on it yet. Leave that until later. Now, do the rest of your homework for tonight as quickly as possible and just do the homework that is due the next day. This does not mean do it as well as you can. This is not the time to be drawing a masterpiece for your 10 minute Spanish assignment where you are supposed to draw pictures representing your vocab words. Just do your homework as fast as you can without it looking like you did it in 10 minutes at midnight. It's an acquired skill you will hopefully *not* have to develop.

After your homework is done for the given night, follow the instructions you made for yourself to work on your project. Be sure to stay on target with your outlined plan to get the project completed in time. Do not change the plan unless you absolutely have to do so. Remember when I said you don't want "half-asleep-you" making important decisions? You will be working on the project after your other homework for the day is completed so you may be a little tired while working on the project. It's true. However, you already have the plan outlined so there won't be much actual thinking and decision-making involved at this point. As you've already made the major strategic decisions, you just need to implement your plan and hopefully still get a reasonable amount of sleep. Even though I've shared my tips for digging out of a hole like this, don't put yourself in the position to need this advice.

To keep from having to scramble to do your projects and homework too late at night, develop good time management habits. First, write down your homework assignments at school in a planner. Some schools give out a school planner at orientation. Use that. This way you won't forget to do your homework and not realize until you are in class that you forgot to do the assignment. Not a good feeling. Next, actually do your homework. This is the most important part. As much as it sucks, you signed up for these classes so now you have to do the work. If you want less work, take easier classes. You might have to give up going out with your friends on some days because you have homework, but in the end, it's worth it. Hopefully you will finish your work by 10:00 p.m. and you can do whatever you want with the rest of the night. Now is the time to watch your favorite TV show, but not before the homework is done. Or you could actually try to get some sleep, which is usually the right decision. Sleep is really, really important.

One important part of managing your time is to do the work needed to successfully complete the assignment, but not do too much more than what is needed. Don't spend an hour on a simple task that should only take fifteen minutes. You could spend that lost time to get ahead on bigger projects or actually doing something enjoyable instead of homework. This seems like common sense but following this rule will ensure you don't fall behind on long term projects because you are eating up your homework time on extra, possibly unnecessary work.

For long projects, don't leave it all to the last minute. Do a little of it at a time. If you have two weeks to complete a project, work 10-20 minutes every day and you will easily finish with time to spare. I promise it's much better to do it that way than to be scrambling to complete the work at 2 a.m. the night before it's due. You will be shocked how easy projects will feel if your work is properly paced. Time management is the most important predictor of doing well in school because it makes the difference between being awake at 2 a.m. and being asleep because you did all of your work ahead of time. It may suck to have to miss out on going out with your friends, but wouldn't you rather not have to cram all your homework into one night?

In addition, be aware of how much work you have and how long this will take and plan your days accordingly. If you have evening commitments such as a sport or work, get some school work done beforehand and, if you can't, be prepared for long nights. For example, I have an hour-long car ride to and from soccer practice twice a week. Fortunately, my mom or one of the other moms drives our carpool. I typically use this time doing whatever homework can be done in a car, such as reading for English or typing an essay on a laptop. Of course, I would rather spend this time relaxing and listening to music, but I know I need to get work done during this valuable time if I want to go to sleep before midnight. Doing work in the car is not the most fun thing I could be doing, but it's necessary if I want to do well in school. Remember, these are the classes you chose to take and all classes come with work, some more than others. If you want to take the Honors English class, expect a lot of work. It is called "honors" for a reason.

Compared to middle school, high school comes with a lot more homework, but it not impossible to complete. If you leave it all to the last minute, it will seem insurmountable, but you're not going to do that, right? If you can't tell, I've done this to myself and it's horrible. Ask anyone in high school; it's happened to just about everyone and it's miserable. So, be smart and learn from my experience to manage your time well. Basically, just pace yourself and don't procrastinate and you'll be fine.

Tip #4:
Get Involved in School

*S*chool isn't just a place where you go to learn for six hours and then go home, do homework, and go to sleep. Done correctly, high school is a place where you foster your passions and look forward to going every day. At least, that is how it should be. The sad reality is that most high schools aren't really like that and require you to use your positive attitude to make it all it can be. You can do that by getting involved in clubs, interest groups, or school sports. These are great ways to feel connected to your school and to your classmates. See what clubs your school offers. You will probably be amazed at the variety of options. My school even has a Dungeons and Dragons club. Trust me, there is something for you. And if there isn't, start your own club. Some examples of clubs I've heard about are: American Cancer Society, Dungeons and Dragons, Girl Up, Relay For Life, California Scholarship Foundation, Mock Trial, Gay-Straight Alliance, Equestrian Club, Fashion Club, Model United Nations, Speech and Debate, Robotics Club, and so many more.

Whatever your interest, you can probably find a club or interest group on that topic or start one of your own. Starting a club is usually pretty easy and also provides an opportunity for you to take a leadership role in your school. For example, I founded a club at my school called Students Helping Students when I realized a need for a resource for my peers who were struggling to find help when dealing with challenging situations and it was a great way to support my school community. Whether you join an existing club or create an entirely new one, you will meet people who have similar interests as you, making it more likely you'll make friends with similar values and interests. Some clubs meet during lunch and others meet after school so it's usually possible to find something that fits into your schedule. I've found clubs to be a great way to get involved not only at school, but also in the community.

If joining a club doesn't interest you, another way to make friends with similar values and interests is to become a student-athlete. There is a long list of sports offered at most high schools and, for the most part, you don't need much experience, especially freshman year. Depending on the competition for the given sport, there is a good chance that if you try out, even if you have no experience, you will at least make Frosh-Soph. Sports offered at most schools can include football, basketball, lacrosse, volleyball, soccer, tennis, cheerleading, dance team, water polo, and swim team. Check them out and see if one of them is right for you.

If nothing I've mentioned so far interests you, you could join student government. They plan school rallies, fundraisers, and dances and always seem to have food at their meetings. It looks pretty enjoyable, but it's not for everyone.

This may not fit into the category of getting involved in school, but I recommend that you go to your school dances. They are great excuses to get dressed up and have a good time with your friends. Some schools focus on having a date, but it's really not a big deal to go without one. It's fun either way. I missed my Winter Formal freshman year, and I really regret not going because my friends told me what a great time they had. My sophomore year, I went to

Homecoming and it was a great experience. I don't really know how else to say this, but just go. You'll have fun.

Going to school can feel like going to prison for six hours every day, but it doesn't have to be that way. Clubs, interest groups, student government, sports, and dances are enjoyable and make school just a little bit more bearable. They are a great way to leave a lasting influence on your school and community and let you explore a topic in which you have interest. And, honestly, since you have to go to school for the required parts, you would be smart to take advantage of the extra-curricular aspects of school as well.

Tip #5:
Don't Get Caught Up in Drama

I know it might seem like an argument with your best friend is the worst possible thing, or that it's the end of the world if that one girl you hate is dating the guy you like, or that it's important to get involved in every conflict at school, but it's usually not. Try not to get sidetracked by all the drama. Think of it this way: in ten years, will any of this really matter? Most of the time, no.

My advice is to just stay out of things that don't actually involve you. There is no reason for you to make it your business. If the people involved want your opinion, they will ask for it. If not, it is in your best interest to mind your own business. It's not your drama so don't make it that way.

Next, don't ruin friendships over the stupidest little thing. It's not worth it. If your friend says something you don't like, settle it like the mature high schooler I'm sure you are. Don't come up with some petty plan to get revenge. It's a waste of time and really immature. It might seem like if you get in one argument, you will never be friends again, but in reality, you will probably make up and go back to being best friends the next day as long as you don't make it a bigger deal than it is. Just use your kindness and compassion to talk directly to your friend. Realize that usually it is more important to maintain the friendship than win the argument. There is an old saying that you can be right or you can be happy, but usually you can't be both. Try to be the friend who puts friendship and happiness above being "right" by letting the small stuff go.

On the flip side, don't be the friend who gets angry over every little thing. It's really annoying. You know that one friend who reads too much into every situation and makes a big deal over nothing? Don't be that person. Find friends who really care about you and have your back. Stay with those friends and you will have a lot less drama in your life.

Next, does it really matter that much who is dating whom? Again, in ten years, this will not matter. Unless you are the rare high school sweethearts who end up getting married, and believe me, it's unlikely, you will look back on your high school relationships and be pretty embarrassed. In no way am I saying not to date in high school, but don't get so worried about who is dating whom. It really doesn't matter. If you like this one guy and the girl you hate starts dating him, sure it's OK to feel jealous and maybe a little angry, but don't let it consume you to the point where you're sacrificing your life because of it. Don't get caught up in trying to make him jealous or in doing something hurtful to your nemesis. It's not worth it. Just do your thing and if it's meant to happen, it will and if not, it won't. I know of just one married couple who met in high school. Yeah, one. Life after high school exists.

Gossip is probably one of the worst ways you can waste your time. Why talk about someone else's life when you have one to live yourself? Most gossip doesn't affect you. There are far more important things to think about and talk about than gossip. So what if those two people got into some argument over this thing? It doesn't affect your life. I know it's normal to get caught up in talk about someone else's life. I do it too. Just don't live vicariously through someone else and live your entire life for gossip. Live your own life; not someone else's. Also, don't be the drama queen who makes things up just to spread rumors because they don't have anything better to do. Just don't.

You have so much more to focus on in high school far beyond the drama. Cut toxic people out of your life and focus on making your life better, not worse. Instead of wasting your time spreading rumors, join a club or do anything constructive. It's a much better use of your valuable time. I'm sure you have experienced some of what rumors and gossip can do to people in middle school and in high school it just gets worse. Be kind to everyone you meet, stop focusing on other people's lives, and live a good one yourself. School is hard enough without gossip ruining people's lives.

Tip #6:

Remember to Have Fun

*T*here was a reason I told you to join clubs or sports, not focus on drama, and to practice effective time management. Following these tips will make school – and life - more enjoyable in general. Make time for friends because, while high school may seem like the most stressful time of your childhood, it is somehow also the most carefree. Don't forget to take breaks between schoolwork, clubs, sports, and jobs to do something you truly love. Remember, you are technically still a kid and you deserve to have some fun. My advice is to spend quality time with your friends, and don't make your life revolve entirely around academics.

You only get to experience high school once, so make it count. It would just be sad if all you have to remember from these high school years are memories of homework and studying. Watch the TV show you've been dying to start, go to the party you really want to attend, read a book if you like reading, and generally enjoy life. Have some fun and don't worry too much. Basically, just don't take everything so seriously and do something with your life. It'll make you a much happier person in general and will make the people around you happier as well. Happiness is contagious that way.

In case you want a place to start, here is a list of my recommendations for TV shows, movies, books, and things to do, as well as a short synopsis of each.

TV Shows:

Grey's Anatomy: A drama show that follows young doctors and their lives as they complete their internship, residency, and become attending doctors. Their lives are very eventful and compelling to watch.

Criminal Minds: One of my favorite show of all time. It follows a branch of the FBI called the Behavioral Analysis Unit as they use psychological profiling to catch serial killers.

The Vampire Diaries: A fantasy show that follows Elena Gilbert, a girl who discovers that vampires Stefan and Damon Salvatore have moved to her town. It's hard to explain, but it's a pretty good show.

Quantico: Not a well-known show, but really good. There are two time periods in the first season: one where a group of recruits are being trained for positions in the FBI and another where the main character, Alex Parish, is suspected of being a terrorist. The question of the show is whether she is a traitor or is being framed.

Glee: A group of outcasts from high school form a Glee Club, or competitive show choir, where they compete in competitions and make friendships. It's great if you love music and cheesy high school shows.

Friends: I'm sure you know the general synopsis, but it follows a group of friends, of course, as they live their entertaining lives as cool twenty-somethings in Manhattan in the 1990's. Especially entertaining once you realize how simple life was before cell phones, texting and social media.

Movies:

Revenge of the Bridesmaids - Comedy: The main characters are invited to be bridesmaids at the wedding of their childhood friend who is marrying one of their ex-boyfriends.

Speech and Debate – Comedy: Not a very well-known movie but well worth seeing. Follows the lives of three high school students as they try to stop oppression in their high school.

Pitch Perfect – Comedy: College student Beca wants to move to Los Angeles to be a music producer, but her family requires that she first attend the college where her father works. She joins a competitive acapella singing group, but must completely reform the group's outdated sound if they want to win.

The Hunger Games - Dystopian/Action: Katniss Everdeen volunteers to compete in the annual battle royal in place of her younger sister, where the last kid alive wins.

Star Wars - Sci-Fi: Luke Skywalker must learn to master his Jedi powers in a world where Darth Vader serves as a tyrant. Luke's mission is to rescue Princess Leia and defeat Darth Vader.

Harry Potter - Fantasy: Harry Potter is an orphan who finds out on his eleventh birthday that he is one of the most famous wizards in the world and is going to attend Hogwarts, a school of Witchcraft and Wizardry.

Books:

Divergent – Dystopian: Beatrice Prior lives in a dystopian world in which sixteen-year-olds choose the faction, based on their personality trains, in which they want to live for the rest of their lives. Beatrice must come to terms with who she is and learn to survive in this society.

The Darkest Minds – Dystopian: In a world where the majority of people have been killed by a major disease and survivors develop special powers, Ruby is placed in an internment camp from which she escapes only to find herself on the run from the government.

City of Bones – Fantasy (The Mortal Instruments Series): When her mother is kidnapped by one of the most dangerous men alive, Clary Fray learns she is a Shadowhunter who lives to defeat demons and protect the world.

The Fault in Our Stars – Contemporary: A story about two teenagers with cancer, Hazel Grace and Augustus, who fall in love while on a trip to Amsterdam to meet Hazel's favorite author.

The Selection – Dystopian: Follows America Singer, low in the caste system, who is given the chance of a lifetime: the opportunity to be chosen to compete in the Selection, sort of a Bachelor-style way of choosing the next queen.

Legend — Dystopian: June, a prodigy of the Republic's military, is chosen to find and arrest Day, the most wanted criminal in the country.

The Program- Dystopian: In a world where depression is viewed as a contagious disease, teenagers try to avoid being trapped in a government created "Program" that is meant to cure those suffering from depression. Slone, the main character, thinks The Program is a dangerous experiment and will stop at nothing to avoid it.

Fun things to do:

Go ice skating or roller skating: Depends on the season, but an excellent way to hang out with friends and have a good time.

Go exploring: Find a deserted area (beach, forest, park, etc.) to explore and take pictures with your friends.

Go to an amusement park: Costs a significant amount of money so you can't do this very often, but can be a really pleasant way to spend a day with your friends. If there is one close to you, consider getting an annual pass which will make this more economical if you go often.

Have a movie night at home: Choose from the suggestions above. Get some snacks and stay in.

Join a sports team: Doesn't have to be a travel team, but it can be a good way to make friends, get some exercise, and have fun.

Volunteer: Find a cause you believe in and volunteer there. Some options could be for a charity or animal shelter.

Go Swimming: Always a fun thing to do but depends on the season. Have a swim party with a bunch of friends or go to the beach if you live near one.

Tip #7:

Don't Worry Too Much About Your Future

*Y*eah, I know. High school is the four years that basically determine if you will have a successful future or not. I get it. If you don't do well in high school, you won't get into the right college and if you don't get into that college, you won't get the right job and if you don't get that job, your life will be unsuccessful. This might be true, but probably not.

It might seem like if you get one "B" in high school your entire future will be ruined, but that's simply not true. Your life will go on. Sure, maybe you could have gotten an "A" in that class if you had worked harder, but at what cost? You can't spend every hour of your life studying from the moment you wake up until the second you go to sleep. It's physically impossible and trying to study at this pace this will probably make you have a complete mental and physical breakdown. Especially freshman year, if you get a "B" or even a "C", it's really not the end of the world.

This kind of ties in to the concept of choosing the courses that are right for you. If you take the most challenging courses in which you can still do well, you will likely end up in a pretty good position.

I know there's always going to be that one student in each of your classes who is a literal genius and seems to easily breeze by tests that are so difficult for you. Maybe you stayed up until 3 a.m. the night before the test studying and still got a "B" when this person seemed to barely study and got an "A". I know, these people suck. However, I promise you that person likely studied a lot harder than they want anyone to know. Regardless, stop comparing

45

yourself to them. There is always going to be someone who does better than you. That's life. Instead of comparing yourself to these people, compare yourself to your own best self. Do the best you can do and accept the results. The less you compare yourself to others, the happier and more successful you're likely to be. I know it's hard to hear but you have to hear it from someone. It's better it's me because you don't know me. You can say I'm completely wrong and I'll never know. You do you. Just know these people who "never study" probably don't have social lives and rarely sleep because of how many hours a day they study. They just don't want you to know how hard they work, because they want you to think everything comes easily to them. See, I just revealed their secret. And if you are one of these people: see, I just figured you out.

Remember to live your life and not someone else's life and that one grade is not the most important thing in the world. What would your life be without any social life? Boring and unhappy. That's what it would be. Sure you could be spending your time studying instead of going to your friend's birthday party, but is it really worth it? Again, think about your life in ten years. Will you remember the grade you got on that test or memories from your friend's birthday party? Now think about high school. Do you really want to remember studying and that's it? No. You don't. You want to remember having fun with your friends and making memories and friendships that will hopefully last a lifetime. Remember you only get to experience high school once, so instead of only living to have the future you want, live to have a great life now. Not later.

I completely understand the constant stress about the future. It's scary not to know where you will be or what you will be doing in just four years. It's even more scary that a couple of bad grades you earn over the course of four years while you are a teenager are going to partly determine your future success. I know ignoring this stress feels like you are saying you don't care about your future, but hear me out. I understand the pressure from your parents who always seem to want to talk about college and career paths. In a way, having a college in mind or career path as a goal can actually cause even more stress because now you know exactly how well you need to do to make your dreams a reality. It's almost easier not to have a definitive career path or dream college in mind. At this point in life, it's better to focus on where you are and do the best you can while still enjoying your life.

Sometimes I feel like high school is a sort of state of limbo. Everyone wants to focus on the future, as if nothing you are doing now affects your immediate life, and in a way, it doesn't. If you get a "C" in math, it really won't affect your life until senior year when college applications are the most important thing in your life. Or at least that's what you're told should be the most important thing in your life.

I think that's why high school students place so much value on gossip and drama. It's really the only thing we can do that actually impacts our immediate life; the here and now. When you are an adult, drama isn't as important because everything else you do affects your current life. In high school, drama often seems like the only thing we can do that actually affects anything now. However, is it? Actually, not. There's so much right now that you can be doing that can positively impact your life and the lives of those around you. That's where your focus should be right now. Focus on how you can make life better today and focus less on the future. Which club can you start or join? Which interesting job could you find for this summer? Which book will you read next? Which new friend can you make at school? These are the elements of life that you can directly impact today and which also have the potential for the most future impact on your life and that is where you should put your focus and attention.

Sometimes you just need to step back and realize that your future isn't the only thing that matters. Try your best to enjoy your high school journey, live a good life, and make lasting friendships in addition to working hard in school. While friendships don't necessarily make your college applications any stronger, they sure do make life a whole lot better. So, stop only worrying about tomorrow and spend more time on what's important today.

Tip #8:

Don't Do Something Just Because Everyone Else Is

*T*his concept can be applied to any number of aspects of your life. Maybe this relates to relationships and dating, which is probably the first thing that popped into your head when you read this tip. Maybe it's about drugs and alcohol. Maybe it's about which classes to take. Maybe it's about extracurricular activities. Maybe it's all of them.

For dating, the simplest application of this rule is: don't date if you don't want to. If you don't want a boyfriend or girlfriend, just don't have one. Don't be afraid to politely say "no" if someone asks you out, regardless of what other people think. Don't feel pressure from others, whether it be your friends or the person who wants to date you. If your friends are pressuring you to do something you don't want to do, then they really aren't good friends. If someone is pressuring you to date them against your wishes, then they aren't worth your time.

Along the same lines, if you are dating someone and they want you to do something you don't feel comfortable doing, don't do it. It's your body and you get to decide what you do and don't want to do with it. Don't feel like you need to go along with what everyone else is doing. Sometimes the most powerful and important thing to say is "no." Spend time figuring out your core values and then live those values. Say "yes" if something is consistent with your values and "no" if it's not. It is perfectly acceptable to say "no" if you just don't feel comfortable in a situation.

For example, if you are at a party and someone pulls out a bottle of vodka, what would you do? I know it's a pretty difficult situation, but it's one that you may encounter in the coming years. If you drink it, you are going against your values (at least, I hope this would be going against your values) and quite literally, the law. However, if you don't drink it, you risk being called a prude and possibly being teased by everyone else at the party. On the surface, it seems like a lose-lose situation. Remember this, never feel pressure to drink alcohol. Don't go against your beliefs just because everyone else is doing it and you want to fit in. It's not worth it. Is fitting in that important? It's more important to stay true to your values than to risk compromising them to fit in with everyone else. If you need help getting out of the situation, call someone you trust, whether it's a parent or close friend, and ask them to come get you. I recommend telling your fellow partygoers that you're sick. Consider having a code to use when you call someone for help. For example, you can have an agreement with your parents that you can call and say "I feel nauseous" when you're in a bad situation. Your parents will know that means to come get you immediately, no questions asked. This sort of agreement can also build trust between you and your parents. They know they can trust you to call them when you're in trouble and you know you can trust them to come get you without punishment.

Anyone who mocks you for being a "prude" is simply not a good friend. Would you ridicule one of your close friends? I hope not. Please don't. This also applies to drugs. They are not good for you. Don't do them. If the people around you think it's "cool" to get high on weekends, they probably aren't the kind of people you want to be around. They could be spending their time doing something useful, but instead, they are getting high or drinking their problems away. Don't be like them. Trust me, you don't want to be like that. If you give in just one time, it could turn into another time, and then a third, and before you know it, you are addicted to something you only tried to be cool. Don't do it.

On a much lighter note, don't take a certain class just because everyone else is doing it or because it is on the path everyone says you should be on. This ties into taking the classes that are right for you. Don't let anyone else decide which classes you should take. They are not the ones doing the work or receiving the grade.

Similarly, don't play a sport, join a certain club, or do anything just because everyone else is. If you really want to try out for lacrosse, but everyone says you should do baseball, think long and hard before going against your own instincts. Do what inspires you. In this situation, if you play baseball and you really hate it, you likely will have a pretty miserable season. My guess is that you'll be a lot happier and more fulfilled playing the sport that you love.

Along the same lines, don't join a club just because your parents say it will look good on your college application. Yes, it is a good idea to join clubs to make friends with people with similar interests, but don't join a certain club if it doesn't appeal to you. I'm sure your parents will understand. Say your parents want you to join Knitting Club (I'm completely making this up, by the way) and you truly have no interest in knitting. Let's say you would much rather join the Robotics Club. Join Robotics Club. Ultimately you will get a lot more out of activities where you have a lot of genuine interest. And when you tell your parents you don't want to join Knitting Club, learn from my experience and don't yell at them. I promise it won't go well. Just say you are interested in something else, make the case for why this is a good use of your time and your parents will probably support you.

And, as far as college applications go, I'm told that it just matters if you show you are interested in something and show commitment and passion for your interests. Colleges can tell if you are genuinely interested in something or if you are just doing it for an application. So, follow your passion, whether it is a sport, chess competitions, or training service dogs and don't worry about how that will affect your college applications.

The bottom line, though, is don't volunteer somewhere or get a certain job or do anything else along these lines because you are told you "should." There are an endless number of things people say you should do and if you did them all, you'd have no time left for what you actually enjoy and value. And that would make your life pretty miserable. Except you do have to go to school. I know you might have a lot of other things you'd rather do, and so do most teenagers, but it's kind of required by law and you'd get in trouble if you don't go to school. Sorry.

Tip #9:
Find Extra-Curricular Activities
You Actually Enjoy

*Y*eah, high school is difficult and time consuming. But that doesn't mean your entire life should revolve around school. It is still important to do something you love. I'm sure in middle school you did something you enjoyed outside of school such as a sport, musical instrument, or volunteering so try to stay involved in those activities. If not, then maybe I can inspire you to find something else you enjoy doing.

Most schools offer extracurricular activities whether they be electives or after school. However, you probably don't want to be at school all day so you may want to find something outside of school where you can also make friends from other schools. It's important to have a life outside of school. It's worth it.

I've played soccer for eight years and it's something that makes me who I am. Find something you care about enough to give up sleep and your free time to do. One of my teachers said something to me that really stuck with me. When a classmate asked me why I would wake up at 4 a.m. to drive three hours to play a soccer game, my teacher said: "It's because she really loves soccer and when you love something, you sacrifice for it."

My teacher's comment really made me think about how I choose to spend my free time. If you're not willing to sacrifice for something, should you really be doing it? Ask yourself this when you are deciding what to do with your time. And when you find something you really love, don't let it go.

It is so important to find something you love because it will bring joy to your life and this joy will spread to others. Also, commitments outside of school will teach you to prioritize and manage your time. For example, if I have to leave for practice at 5 p.m. and won't get back home until 9 p.m., I've learned to get as much homework done as possible before I leave. Sometimes I get work done in the car so I won't need to stay up so late to finish. You might question why I committed so much time to soccer. I did it because I love the sport of soccer. Try to find something you love that much. Try to find something you are willing to give up sleep to do.

Which is your favorite activity outside of school? It could be volleyball, football, baseball, soccer, lacrosse, water polo, dance, piano, guitar, drums, flute, volunteering at an animal shelter, volunteering at a church, joining an academic team, or many more possibilities. You get the point. There are so many great activities out there. Find one or more that's right for you.

It's worth your time to spend at least a couple hours a week doing something you enjoy outside of school. Have a life that doesn't just revolve around school. School can sometimes be boring. Don't make it your whole life. Find something you like doing and stick with it, no matter how hard school gets. It gives you a much-needed break from endless studying and tests. We all need breaks in our busy lives.

Tip #10:
Try To Understand What Your Teachers Want From You

*T*his is probably something you got a taste of in middle school, but it's one of the most important tools in high school; second only to headphones. Headphones are your best friend at school, and you will probably figure out why within the first couple of weeks. Getting back on topic, try to figure out your teachers within a couple of days in their class. Try to see what they like and what they don't like, how much time and effort they expect you to put into the class, and what they're looking for from you.

At first, this seems like a difficult skill to master, but in reality, it's pretty easy. Let's start with figuring out what they like and what they don't like. This mostly applies to classes where you will be writing, but it can apply to other classes as well. For English, teachers usually will have you write about yourself or give some kind of writing assignment to start off the year. Take this as a trial run. Use your normal writing style and see how it is received. If you do well on the assignment, you know you are all set. If you don't, you know where you need to improve because most teachers will leave comments. Don't feel all cocky and pretend your teacher doesn't know anything or grades too hard. They do know something, otherwise they wouldn't be a teacher and sure, maybe they may grade a little too hard, but there are always going to be teachers like that. It sucks, but deal with it. It's only a year. Use the teacher's constructive criticism and learn from it. Maybe your teacher is impressed by bigger words or prefers a certain writing style. Try your best to write as well as you can, while at the same time making small adjustments to account for what your teacher wants to see in your work. Once you've figured out your teacher's preferences, writing in that class will be so much easier. For example, once I had an English teacher who required that we start and end all of our sentences with nouns. She also banned a lot of common words and phrases that students use all of the time. If you end up having a teacher like mine, it may not make sense, I know, but it's best to follow your teacher's directions if you want to get the best possible grade. And you may also learn something along the way that makes you a better writer. Don't be so stubborn; adapt your writing style, if necessary.

Ok, now you've learned how to figure out what your teacher likes and doesn't like to see when grading. Next, I am going to teach you how to figure out how much time you should put into a class. Don't tell me some cliché about how you should never skimp on your work and it should always be great. Yes, that's the ideal but sometimes the ideal isn't possible because you only have a certain amount of time for homework and studying and you will likely have to make hard choices on how to allocate your time. If one teacher is known for grading on the easier side, you may not need to do extra work in that class. You may want to spend that freshly available time on homework for other classes where the teacher may be a tougher grader. There's always going to be a class that's pretty easy for you and another that requires a little more work. Smart students allocate their homework time accordingly. Early in the school year you will learn if your teacher grades very strictly or if the class is fairly easy for you and may not require as much work. Use that information to budget your time and increase the likelihood you will do well.

There's always going to be the class where it seems like you need to spend ten hours a day to do well. Spend your extra time working at that class as this is where the extra time and effort will really pay off.

Learn what classes are easier for you and require less work and focus on the classes that require more work and plan your time accordingly. It's as simple as that.

The last thing about figuring out your teachers is figuring out to make a good impression on them. If you make a good impression on a teacher, they're more likely to be understanding and supportive even if you struggle in the class. They may also be more likely to offer you extra credit or extra tutoring, which can only help you. To do this, be sure to make a good first impression on the first day of school. Keep your head down and don't chat with your friends during class or do anything that will make the teacher hate you because first impressions are where they choose the students they don't like. Don't be that student. After the first day is over, start participating in class and asking questions. Most teachers love to teach, so if you show genuine interest in their class or show how you are willing to work to do well, the teacher will like you a lot more. The worst way for a teacher to feel about you is to be indifferent. You want the teacher to know who you are and to think well of you. The students who keep to themselves and don't participate in class are rarely the students the teachers like very much. It's actually not that they actively dislike these students. They just don't really know who they are so they're not on the teacher's radar for good or bad. You don't want that. You want to be on the teacher's radar in a good way.

So, ask questions and show your teachers that you want to be a good student and learn what they are trying to teach. That helps to make a good, lasting first impression.

Tip #11:
Try Something New

*H*igh school is a time for new experiences and new opportunities. Take advantage of it. You never know if you might really enjoy doing something until you try it. That may be a cliché, but that's because it's true. Try not to turn down opportunities to try something new and interesting because you may be missing out on something that could become your passion. Think of things that you love doing that you couldn't imagine not being a part of your life. Now imagine your life without those things. Pretty boring, right? That's what your life might be like if you never tried those things. You don't want that, right? No, you don't.

Whether it be academic or extracurricular, try new things. Find a new hobby, try a new sport, take a class in which you think you might have interest. I'm not saying you should try things you're not likely to like. You know yourself better than anyone else so don't waste your time trying something you know you're not likely to enjoy. On the other hand, be open to trying new things that there's a chance you might like. It may be worth it in the long run.

Conversely, if you try new things, you will also find out what you don't like. I know it's kind of early to be thinking of career paths, and it's really scary to think about that. However, if you can rule out as many options as possible in high school, where the stakes are low, it will make it much easier when you really do need to choose a career; and that day will come. I know, it feels like high school will never end, but it will. And sadly, you will need to join the real world where you will need to go to work and support yourself. Sucks, right? I'm told its much more enjoyable to do something for a living that you actually enjoy and look forward to going to work every day to do. Hence, the reason why you want to figure out what you actually like to do. But isn't it easier to choose from five possible career paths than hundreds? It is, if you didn't know. It really is.

Remember my story about trying that video production class? I genuinely thought I'd enjoy the class, but I didn't. It wasn't for me and now I won't have to find this out in college and then have to pick another major. It really is a way not only to save money, but also time.

So, without the added pressure of thinking about your future, try new things to see what you like and what you don't like. It doesn't just have to be in school, it can be in all aspects of life. You can use this idea to see what hobbies are for you and you can also weed out the ones that aren't. It's not the end of the world. You won't lose much time trying them out. And, at minimum you've figured out something you definitely don't want to try again. And, hey, on the off chance you find something you really love, you can thank me. Not really. You can't really talk to me. But you can thank me in theory. or you could even email me. I'd appreciate knowing someone actually read this and took it seriously.

I do really think it's worthwhile to try new things, because you might find the one thing you want to do for the rest of your life. You won't be able to find anything you like without trying it and taking the risk that you won't like it. Imagine if you never ate anything. I know, you'd die if you don't eat, but let's just pretend for a second you'd be fine. If you never ate anything from birth (if you never ate from birth that would mean your parents are pretty heinous parents, but that's another story), you'd never find your favorite food. Yeah, there's probably a long list of foods you don't like. I know, as I'm a pretty picky eater. However, if your favorite food is sushi and you never tried it, you wouldn't know you like it. It's as simple as that. You're welcome.

So, try out for the sport you've been wanting to try, take the class you're hesitant to take, do something you've been thinking about doing, but weren't sure if you would like it. It will be worth it. And anyways, the stakes are pretty low. Maybe you'll like it and maybe you'll hate it. If you hate it, you've ruled out something you might have learned that you hated later in life, when the stakes are higher. And that would suck. You'd be broke and unhappy. And bored. That's a trio you don't want to happen. So don't. Take my advice and don't stay in your safety bubble. Get out of your comfort zone, even if it's just into the kiddie pool. I'll be proud of you. Actually I don't really know who you are, but at least in theory I would be.

Tip #12:
Sleep

I want to take a minute to talk about my amazing best friend. She is there for me when I'm sad and always makes me feel better. When I'm exhausted, she always finds a way to give me the extra energy I need. I don't know where I would be without my best friend: sleep.

Sure, it sounds a little weird to talk about sleep in these terms, but in high school, sleep should be your best friend. If you think you had a lot of work in middle school, I'm sorry to break this to you, but you're very mistaken. Yeah, high school is basically middle school on steroids. It can be fun and all, but it's still a lot of work. Teachers expect you to go to school for six hours and go home and do at least six more hours of homework. They don't seem to know that you have other classes and, I don't know, a life, and will assign hours of homework with no warning. It sucks. However, you can't really complain too much about it because you want your teachers to like you; remember Chapter 10 "Try To Understand What Your Teachers Want From You."

Sometimes I think about what would happen if students went on strike and didn't do their homework. If no one did homework, teachers would stop assigning it, right? I doubt it would work, but it's a cool idea.

So, I have to get back to the point of this chapter. You really need to sleep when you have the opportunity. My school actually used to have a club called the Sleep Appreciation Club. It was a club that met every day at lunch so the members could take a nap. They were disbanded before my freshman year because people didn't wake up on time and were always late to class; most likely because they were so tired from being sleep-deprived. You might wonder how students could be so desperate that they would create a club just so they could sleep, right? However, sometimes, to do well in school, you need to sacrifice everything, even your sleep.

Doctors say teenagers need between 9 to 9 1/2 hours of sleep a night and wonder why we aren't. It's just impossible. To get 9 hours of sleep, a student, let's say his name is Bob, would wake up at 7 a.m., which is pretty late for most students, and would have to go to sleep at 10:00 p.m. Let's assume Bob gets out of school around 3 p.m. and gets home around 3:30 p.m. Let's also assume he doesn't have any sports or anything else that would require him to stay after school. With the six hours of daily homework that students often get, Bob will finish his work around 9:30 p.m. if he starts working the minute he gets home. This leaves Bob just enough time to eat something and go to sleep. That makes no sense. That means Bob's entire life is school, homework, and sleep. That is the only way he could get 9 hours of sleep every night.

Teachers don't see the problem with assigning an hour or more of homework each night. How much could that hurt? But if Bob has 6 classes, which many students do, and they all assign an hour of homework, or if one, just one, assigns 2 or 3 hours of work, that can very quickly add up to more than six hours of work. That's completely ridiculous and not capable with getting a healthy amount of sleep each night.

One way to combat this is to take naps every possible chance you get. Learning to sleep as a passenger in the car can be pretty hard to master, but it's a very important skill. If you have a half hour commute to school, that's half an hour you can add on to your night's worth of sleep. If you have to drive to practice, taking a short nap in the car can make the amount of homework you need to complete seem a little more manageable. Napping isn't procrastinating as sleep is so important to your health and how you feel and you probably wouldn't be doing anything important in the car anyway.

Doctors are now saying kids are getting addicted to caffeine at a younger and younger age, and I can see why. It's because schools are putting so much stress on students at a significantly younger age, making them lose sleep and turn to energy drinks and coffee to stay awake. My brother was just in fourth grade and already learning algebra. In fourth grade, I was basically learning how to multiply. Not really. I'm just exaggerating for effect, but you get the point. Kids are expected to do more and more complex work at a younger and younger age and this adds to their already excessive work load. In some ways, kids are losing part of their childhoods because of this. I may not have the answers to the dilemma, but I want you to understand this problem and that it's something all kids struggle with in modern life.

Basically, what I'm trying to say is to not overburden yourself. Be kind to yourself and don't be so hard on yourself if you don't always do well in every class. It's harder than ever to be a kid these days so don't add more pressure on yourself. Part of this self-kindness means that you need to make sure you get enough sleep. Don't always watch your favorite show and expect to stay awake super late to finish your work. Just go to sleep. The weekends can be a time to catch up. Friday night, you can probably stay up as late as you want and sleep in on Saturday. A lot of times, Thursday night is the night to stay up late because Friday is the day most teachers don't do as much in school; except that one teacher who always schedules tests on Friday. I'm not a big fan of Friday tests in case you can't tell. You can usually make up the sleep over the weekend. Just try to sleep during the week as much as you can and learn to accept that you aren't always going to get the optimal amount of sleep each night. I'm sorry. Someone had to tell you. Go easy on yourself while still doing the best you can. And, if you are reading this over the summer vacation, try to get as much sleep as you can before school starts.

Tip #13:

Find A Passion Outside of School

*T*his kind of goes along with Tip #6: "Remember to Have Fun." Finding your passion is what life is all about. You don't want to just dabble in many things. You want to find your passions and really explore them. Having passions will help you as you move into the future. It will come up on interviews for college, graduate school, jobs, etc. Sorry, we're going to have to talk a little about the future in this chapter. You've been warned.

How do you find your passions? Simply put, you need to try lots of new things until you find what you actually love to do. And if you don't figure it out right away, keep trying. Eventually you will find something you love. Once you find your passions, settle down with them. You will always want to spend lots of time with your passions, although you won't ever want to give up trying new things.

When you find something you love, don't give it up for the next new thing. Make time for it, prioritize it, and get really good at it. Enter some competitions to inspire you to keep with it. It could even teach you something that you could write about in your college essays. Colleges want to see that you have passions and that you can stick with them. It shows that you have discipline and perseverance. Those are two traits colleges want in their students.

One of the more important things I can tell you about finding your "thing" is that it really doesn't matter what it is, unless it is watching Netflix because that won't get you too far. Seriously though, the main thing I can tell you about your passion is that it should be something outside of school. That's what this tip is all about. You don't want your entire life to revolve around school. That's pretty boring. Remember when I told you to have a life outside of school? It's still true. You need somewhere you can go to enjoy yourself that's not school. You also need friends outside of school. That way when there's drama at school, you still have friends you can rant to who will be on your side. They only know one person that's involved; and that's you. That makes it so much better because they will support you no matter what. Sometimes that's just what you need; unconditional support. For me, that thing outside of school is soccer. It has taught me resilience, kept me fit, and helped me make real, life-long friends. It will be something that I have for the rest of my life; something I can do when I have nothing else to do and when I have everything else to do, but don't want to do it quite yet. Find your thing. It makes school so much better. And if you're lucky, you've already found that thing. And if you found that thing in the past and stopped doing it, it's probably not too late to go back and rediscover it.

I've already given you a list of possibilities when I told you about doing something fun outside of school. If you need to review this again, go back to chapter 6 (but probably best not to focus on the TV shows). I'm not going to write about it again here, as there's really no point. However, if you took the time to look at it and remember reading it and thinking, "maybe I'd be good at that," perhaps you should try it. Remember, though, this one shouldn't be at school. I'm talking about passions that are outside of school. That's the most important part.

Another important part about this is that it is your genuine passion. You need something about which you really care deeply. It should be that one thing you would give up anything to do. It should be the thing you would wake up at 4 a.m. to do. Find it and never let it go.

Tip #14:

Get Really Good At Something Academic

Y eah, I know it's good to be a well-rounded student, to know a little of everything. But after nine or more years of being in school, I'm sure you know what subjects you are good at and enjoy and what subjects you are not great at and don't enjoy. So why focus all of your effort on something you're not that good at and probably won't ever use in the future? Instead, turn your attention to something more useful and take classes that both interest you and in which you are likely to excel. These are the classes that will most likely end up being related to your future college major in some way.

In my case, it's psychology and math. These are the two subjects that I love the most. I don't want to burst your bubble about me, but I genuinely love these two subjects. Thus, I'm taking the highest level of psychology I can possibly take. Some people will tell you that this will make your transcript look better and more impressive and all of that stuff, but more importantly, it will help prepare you for what awaits you at college. I'm most likely going to be a psych major, so these AP and IB credits will not only save me money and time, but also better prepare me for the classes I am going to be taking in the future. I don't know if you knew this, colleges will often consider AP classes as equivalent to the basic level of a course. So if you're bilingual, which by the way is so wonderful, you can take the AP or IB test for your second language, if they offer it at your school. If you pass the test, which you probably will, you will likely have fulfilled your college language requirement. Pretty cool.

Try to reach the highest levels of the classes where you excel. Thus, if you are great at writing and want to be an author, you should take all of the creative writing courses offered at your school, as well as the highest level of English possible at your school. This will better prepare you for whatever liberal arts school you will likely attend in the future. If possible, you don't want to be in all CP classes for every subject. Instead, take the CP classes for some classes, but also go to higher levels in the ones where you excel and enjoy the subject. Play to your strengths, but remember not to challenge yourself so much that you are drowning in work.

Maybe you are thinking, "I'm really not that great at any of my subjects." One, I doubt that's true. Two, it might not be a traditional subject. Math, Science, English, and History are the typical subjects that are considered academic. However, there are jobs that don't technically involve any of these. I know it's scary to think about your future, but we're going to have to discuss that here. Don't just limit yourself to the main classes. Maybe you want to be a director or a music producer or work in business. Again, look at the electives to see if any of them interest you at all. You really won't know you are interested in a certain career path unless you try it out. This thing can't be a sport or after school activity, unless that activity is academic. For the vast majority of us, sports will end after high school or college. Most of us are not going to be paid to play a sport;

sorry to break it to you. You need to find something you can do for the rest of your life, something realistic.

Once you find this academic subject, you need to find a way to foster it so that you begin to get really good in this subject. The easiest way to do this is to take as many relevant classes as you can. In addition to this, read about it online. The Internet is not just a place for funny cat videos and Tik Tok (I think that's how it's spelled). If you are interested in the medical field, watch documentaries about health and start reading articles about medical research. Stay informed and look out for possible job opportunities. Job opportunities may simply be volunteer at this stage, but they will still give you worthwhile experience and connections. Internships are how people enter the working world and they can be hard to find. Get really good at talking with professionals so you will be able to do well in interviews once those come your way. One of the keys to interviewing is to show just how passionate you really are about your interests. Don't be afraid to show how much interest you have in things. I know you may not have even started freshman year yet and I'm here talking about college already and you must be thinking that you aren't even close to needing to think about that, but high school is only four years. Four years really isn't that long. It goes by fast. Doing well in high school will set you up for success in college. So, make these four years count and try to set yourself up for a certain career path you can major in in college. If you don't find the thing you want to do, that's totally ok. However, if you do, it's going to be a lot easier for you in the future when everyone has no idea what to do with their life and you already have a direction. You can always change your path so don't worry. Just keep looking for passions and explore those and your career path will eventually make itself clear to you.

Tip #15:
Set Goals For Yourself

I know this sounds really clichéd, but setting attainable goals for yourself will help you out a ton. Don't set goals that are unrealistic and, let's be honest, you know when you have set an unrealistic goal. Don't overestimate yourself, but also don't underestimate yourself. Not everyone is going to go to an Ivy League school or become a professional athlete or discover the cure for cancer so don't expect that of yourself. Simply do the best you can each day and see where that takes you. Maybe it will take you to an Ivy League school. Maybe it won't. Who knows? Strive to be the best you can be without getting too attached to any expectations. Once you've accepted this, life becomes a whole lot less stressful. The weight of expectations is lifted.

Now that I'm done rambling so far off topic, I'm going to go back to talking about setting goals. These goals can be academic or athletic or whatever you want them to be. Yeah, I know some people are going to have their goals to be "finish season seven of Friends by Friday." Ok, that doesn't count. At least if you want to be productive, that doesn't count. Your goals should be something like: get an "A" in AP Euro. Another goal could be to make varsity basketball or be promoted to manager at your job. You may be thinking now that I just said to have no expectations, yet now I'm saying to have goals. This is a key point to understand and it took me a while to get it. Goals are good, expectations are bad. It's good to set goals and strive for them, yet these goals should not be expectations. Expectations imply that we will be sad and depressed if we don't meet them. Goals are simply goals. We can achieve them or not. Set goals, but don't be upset if you don't reach them. That way they aren't expectations.

You can have one main goal or multiple smaller goals. If you want a constant reminder of your goals (which I'll admit can be kind of annoying and sometimes overkill), you can write out a list and put it on your wall or in your binder or something. Remember that these goals should be yours and not someone else's. Live for yourself, not your parents or anyone else. If you don't want to go to a certain school or play a certain sport, don't. Unless your parents are making you which, in that case, I'm sorry that really sucks. You're likely to be a lot happier when your goals are your goals and not your friends' goals or your parents' goals.

Once you decide what your goals are, you need to try to achieve them. Instead of watching the show you love on Netflix, spend that extra hour studying or working out or actually working to achieve your goals. These hours really count and this is coming from someone who loves watching Netflix. You really need to put in the extra work if you want to get what you say you want. Think of it this way: many people are lazy, including me sometimes, so if you work harder than everyone else, you can catch up to and surpass people who become complacent or just don't want to put in the work. You will be amazed how much you can accomplish with steady, consistent work toward your goals.

If you have that one killer class, and we all know what class just kills us, spend extra time studying for it or get extra help. I know it can be embarrassing, but if you have a friend who understands something that is a struggle for you, ask them for help. They will usually be happy to help unless you are always asking them for help without trying to figure it out first. Swallow your pride and ask them. And then offer to help that person with something that causes them to struggle. Be the kind of person who gives help to others. Offer to tutor those who need help in the area where you excel. And, take advantage of your school's tutoring center and of any times your teacher makes themselves available to offer extra help to students. There's no shame in getting extra help and teachers actually like it when they see that something isn't easy for you and that you are still working as hard as possible.

Also, I know exercise is not always fun, but spend time exercising and set goals for your physical fitness level. Even if you don't play a sport, getting in shape can make you a happier and healthier person and it is a great way to take a break from school. If you do play a sport, it is a great way to become better conditioned and increase your strength which will make you play better. You can make it an activity to do with your friends too. Another perk of working out is you can physically see how you are improving. Seeing yourself get stronger is a great motivator to keep exercising.

Setting goals for yourself will force you to address what you actually want to be doing in the future as well as giving yourself something to work towards, because in reality if you are not working towards something, why are you working on it at all? High school can be a scary place because everything you do will matter so much in a few years when you are applying to college. This can be frightening if you think about it so try not to think too much about this right now. Instead, try to focus on just doing the best you can today. After you do the best you can today, then do the best you can tomorrow, and so on and so on as you move towards your goals. Focusing on doing your best today is the best way to feel less stressed about the future.

As far as your goals go, the most important thing about setting goals is to make sure that they are realistic, which means they are achievable. You will be so stressed out if your goals are impossible to attain. I completely understand how difficult that stress can be so don't let that happen. Set achievable goals and then do your best to reach them without expectations. This will help you to actually succeed.

Tip #16:
Social Media

$\mathcal{S}$ ocial media can be both amazing and horrible at the same time. It is a great way to stay connected with friends and family, especially the ones you don't see on a regular basis. However, social media can also be a huge stressor. In the social media world in which we live, most everything that we post in available for public viewing. Think about that, when you post something or when you do something that can be recorded by someone else. It can be posted online and live on forever. That's terrifying, but it is reality.

The saddest thing is that some people use social media in truly despicable ways to bully others behind the safety of their digital screens. They use these sites to feel powerful, when in their normal lives they may be powerless. They feel like nothing they do online can possibly impact someone's real life but, of course, it can and does. Look at the case of Amanda Todd. Bullies used Facebook to impersonate her and harass her even when she switched schools. Eventually, she committed suicide and now that is something these bullies will live with forever. However, it is too late for her, her friends, and her family

I want to remind you that if social media is providing so much stress that you are having panic attacks or worrying about it every day, consider getting rid of it. You do not need social media if it is providing that much of a negative impact on your life.

Right now, the popular social medias for teenagers are Snapchat and Instagram. I'll address them separately because they are very different.

First is Snapchat. This is the less formal, but potentially more embarrassing social media. Everything you post disappears immediately after it's opened and everything on your story disappears after 24 hours, and you are notified if someone screenshots your picture. These elements of Snapchat make this form of social media the one that tends to be used by people to text things they wouldn't want to live on forever. This is where people send inappropriate and/or embarrassing photos because they think that's it's not permanent. This is also where people can send direct messages to others which delete immediately after the person reads them and closes the message. However, I'm here to tell you that Snapchat provides a false sense of security with the idea that everything you do is temporary and has no long-term effects when in reality, that is simply not the case. Just look on the Internet at everything that can go wrong with Snapchat, because I do not have enough space to address all of them in this book.

Here are some basic rules for Snapchat and other types of social media. Don't post anything online that you wouldn't want everyone in the world to see. If you don't want others to see it, don't post it anywhere. Snapchat has a server where they save everything that is sent or posted and they can retrieve it if necessary. Are you now thinking about that really ugly photo of you that you posted last year and then deleted? Don't worry, they only look on the server in dire situations such as when a crime has been committed. There's been a lot of press recently about posting inappropriate (meaning nude) photos so it's important that we discuss this here. Let me be very clear. Never, ever post an inappropriate photo. Never, ever receive an inappropriate photo from someone else. If you receive something like this, whether via Snapchat or text, tell your parents immediately so they can help you figure out what to do. The laws related to this vary from state to state, but sending or receiving such photos can be a serious crime so just never, ever do it. Remember when you are applying for a job, they may do a background check and can easily find that. So, don't do it. It's really stupid.

Now that we've covered that, we can look at the positive aspects of Snapchat. It can be a convenient way to have contact with your friends and family, especially those whom you don't see on a regular basis. It can be a great way to show your friends what you are doing or where you are on a given day. For example, you can have streaks on Snapchat. This means that if you send or receive messages from the same person every day consecutively, you will have a "streak" with that person. The number of days of your streak will show up next to their name. That is kind of a cool thing to have with a person.

Snapchat can be entertaining, but don't have it if you do not want it. In more general terms, do not do anything on Snapchat, or any social media, that you don't want to do. A good rule is to only do something online that you would be comfortable doing in public or having go viral across the Internet. Just a friendly reminder to think for yourself and act responsibly at all times.

Let's now discuss the other major social media platform: Instagram. This is the more formal social media where people post less frequently and mainly post about where they are. A lot of people will have multiple accounts on Instagram. Typically, they will have a "main" account where they let most people follow them. Then they will have a "private" or "spam" account where they only let close friends follow them and post about their thoughts. They may also have a "super-private" account where they only let really close friends follow. Other types of Instagram accounts are fan accounts which is pretty self-explanatory, meme accounts where people post funny pictures or videos, accounts where people sell old clothes, or professional accounts for people who want to be an "influencer."

Now that we have that all established, you do not need to be on Instagram. There is not much drama on Instagram, but it's also not that important for you. Sure, if you want one, have an Instagram account. However, carefully consider this decision. If you prefer to spend your time elsewhere, delete the account and spend your time on more productive activities.

Social media can be a huge stressor as it allows a forum for anonymous cyberbullying, which is not to be taken lightly. On social media, you can be talked into doing something you do not want to do or you can see things that make you feel less confident about yourself. Although there are some benefits to social media, we can live without it and if you find that it is bringing negative emotions into your life, just delete it. Don't give in to peer pressure in any aspect of your life, but especially when the stakes are high. Social media is not for everyone and it may not be for you.

Tip #17:
Dating

I 'm going to try my best to give some general advice on this topic even though I don't really have much personal experience in this area. I'm sure some of you might have dated someone in middle school and thought you were going to be with that person forever. In my experience, those relationships typically break up by the end of freshman year. Maybe you'll be different.

I don't have much experience dating, but I have friends who do. I'm basically going to use their life experiences to try to teach you what I think it important with dating. First, I'm not going to tell you not to date in high school, so if there are any parents reading this to see if they can use what I'm saying to show to their kids, sorry. The truth though is that most high school relationships don't work out for the long-term. On the other hand, I know of some that did. I actually have a friend whose parents met in their sophomore year of high school and are still together. So, don't say you don't want to date someone because it will never work out because it might. On the other hand, it is much more likely that any high school relationship will end and end badly. So, if you don't want to date in high school, don't. Some people don't have time to date and that is a completely valid reason to not date. Remember when I said that you shouldn't be pressured into doing things you don't want to do? Well, this is another example. If you don't feel that you're ready to date, don't date. There will likely be plenty of time for this down the road.

One important point is that you should not stay in a relationship that you know isn't right for you. I have a friend who was in a relationship for 10 months with this jerk who was controlled everything she did and told her who she could and couldn't hang out with. She stayed with him even after she realized she didn't really want to be with him. After a month of being unhappy, she finally broke up with him and now sees him for who he truly is. What you can learn from this is to get out of toxic relationships and this is something that's better to learn as a teenager than when you are older and the stakes are higher. If you are in a relationship you don't want to be in, get out of it. If you need help in doing this, don't hesitate to enlist your family's help or even seek professional help.

If you do date in high school, use these relationships to learn what you want and what you don't want in a healthy relationship. It's like practicing for when you are older. What do you want in a relationship? This is a good time to start thinking about that. One thing that I know is truly important is that the person makes you feel better about yourself and that you make the other person feel better about himself or herself.

Something else that is really important is to learn is when to say "no." If you don't want to date someone, don't just agree because you feel bad. Instead, you can politely say "no." Don't put yourself in a situation you don't want to be in because you are afraid of letting someone down. If something is happening that you don't want to happen, don't go along with it because you don't want to be seen as different. You are not obligated to do anything. Also, don't get into a relationship because everyone else is doing it and you want to be cool. That's a stupid reason to date someone and it's not fair to the other person.

Another thing I want to add is to date whomever you want. If you are gay, lesbian, bisexual, or whatever, just be yourself. Find relationships where people support you in being who you are. Find people who accept you for you.

Tip #18:
Make Time For Friends

I feel like this is a good topic to cover right after we discussed dating. If you are in a relationship, don't completely isolate yourself from your friends. I've seen people do this and when the relationship breaks up, they are left with no friends and it sucks. I understand that you are going to have to spend less time with your friends when you are in a relationship, but don't make your significant other your only friend. Don't forget your friends.

This topic applies to many situations, not just dating. During the school year, I know some of you will have so much work that you don't even have time to sleep. I can relate. No matter how busy you are, it's important to still make time for friends. Try to find a balance between school and friends. I'm still trying to figure this out myself, but I've learned how important friends are. Boyfriends and girlfriends may come and go, but friends should be forever

I know school can sometimes be overwhelming, but there are ways to set aside time to be with your friends. Try to do some homework before or right after school. Study hall or other breaks during the day can be helpful as well. By getting some of your homework done early in the day, you can to free up time to see your friends. One thing you should avoid doing is to give up your lunch to do homework. That is important free time to hang out with friends and hopefully grab a nutritious meal. Spend your lunch bonding and complaining with your friends about homework you haven't started yet. Those are memories that you will cherish one day.

Occasionally giving up sleep to spend time with friends may be worth it. Most of the time, however, sleep is crucial. You'll feel a lot better when you get sufficient sleep and it's apparently beneficial to good health as well. When you do have time to hang out with your friends, make the most of it. Time with friends is sacred time.

I previously discussed how social media is something that can add stress and negativity to your life. However, there are times where digital technology can enhance your social and academic life. For example, one way to combine school work and socializing is to do homework while on FaceTime with a friend. This works especially well for classes that involve learning a concept and then practicing that concept. Perhaps you and your friend can teach each other the concept on Facetime and then do problems together. This can be a good way to get work done and hang out with a good friend.

I am not telling you to hang out with friends at the expense of compromising your school performance. Life is all about balance. Having friendships improves mental health and happiness and can help us cope with the stress related to school pressures. Taking study breaks to focus on friends or to FaceTime friends while doing homework are great ways to find balance.

Tip #19:

Don't Take Everything So Seriously

*D*o you know someone whose entire life revolves around school, freaks out if they get a "B" on a test, has very few friends, and has essentially no significant extracurricular activities? By the way, I'm sorry if I just described someone you know. However, never fear, I can help.

School is stressful enough these days with kids feeling so much pressure to do well on every test, paper, and class. If you feel stressed about school, first, take a step back and assess the situation. Does one test or one paper really matter that much? I've read many articles and books about very successful, happy people who didn't do well in high school or college and still managed to do very well in life. I have learned that life is a marathon, not a sprint, so try not to get too wrapped up in one situation at school. Try to see the big picture. School does matter, but it is still possible to do well in school even if you bomb one test or paper.

It's also very possible to well in school while still having a healthy social life. I always try to remember that. Many years from now you won't likely remember that test in biology class, but you'll probably remember that day you spent with your friends hanging out at the beach or at the mall.

I see a lot of kids freaking out over every test, assignment, and project related to school. Don't do this. If you don't do well on one test, it's not the end of the world. Try to remember to take a deep breath and relax when things get stressful and you're really worried about a certain test or paper. Remember to "not sweat the small stuff" because ultimately most things are "small stuff" when we look back on them years later. In twenty years, are you still going to be thinking about that test? Probably not.

High school is not meant to be four years of hell so have fun. Go to a few parties, watch a movie with friends, or just hang out with friends and family. Of course, you should still work hard at school, but you also need to take time out for the most important things in your life, your relationships; in particular, your relationships to your family and your friends. These are the most important people in your life. Don't forget that when times get tough and something doesn't go well. During my freshman year, I was worrying about school so much that I did almost nothing for me and that simply made the stress even worse. When we're in stressful situations, we sometimes think that the solution is to simply work harder, when, in fact, the solution is often to take a break and then come back to the situation with a more refreshed outlook. In my sophomore year, I tried seeing friends more often and taking more breaks from schoolwork and I actually ended up doing much better in school and I was also a lot happier.

Schools sometimes don't appreciate how much pressure they put on teenagers. We are given hours of homework to do each day and it has become common for teenagers to have mental breakdowns over school. I've talked to my friends about this and we've realized that this can make students feel stupid or want to drop out of school. That's horrible and please don't feel that way.

During my freshman year, one of my friends was having a rough time at school and started taking an occasional "mental health day" off from going to and studying for school. With parental permission, he picked certain days where he didn't go to school or do any school work. He told me how much it helped him to feel refreshed. Mental health days are actually really important and I hope one day they will be endorsed by schools. Schools accept a student calling in sick for physical reasons, but if someone needs to take a day off because of stress, they are often looked at as weak and usually won't be excused from school. I personally think that makes no sense. I think of it as similar to how certain religions have a "Sabbath" or day of rest. In the modern world, we seem to have forgotten the importance of this, but please remember this idea, especially when things get stressful. Remember to take care of yourself by taking time to recharge.

During these "recharging days," do what you need to do to recharge whether it is sleeping in, reading a book, watching a movie, or just hanging out. One piece of advice about this is to try to spend time with friends and family, if possible, during these recharging days. Being with other people when you're stressed is usually much more helpful than being alone.

So, don't focus all of your time and effort on school because it will wear you out over time. Don't take everything so seriously. Remember to take time to keep yourself refreshed and remember that life is a marathon, not a sprint. This is your life to live and try to see the forest even when the individual trees may be stressing you out.

Tip #20:
Friends and Family Challenges

*T*his is an area where I have some personal experiences that I can share, but I'm going to change names and specific details to protect identities. Family challenges can definitely affect all parts of your life and are something faced by a lot more people than you probably expect. Some of you might have already had family challenges impacting you in middle school, so you've hopefully already figured some ideas of how to live with them. However, some of you might experience this for the first time in high school, and my job is to try to help.

The first time I remember my family affecting my life at school was in third grade. My sister, Clara, had just started first grade and her undiagnosed anxiety was beginning to emerge. She panicked every day she went to school. Just standing outside the entrance to school elicited tremendous anxiety for her. I remember watching her causing a scene in front of school as she struggled with this every day and it was truly heartbreaking. I remember not wanting to get out of the car because it was so painful for me to watch. Looking back now, I wish that I had been more understanding and supportive of her. When you're that young, it's sometimes difficult to show compassion for those who are struggling with mental health issues, but I learned a powerful lesson that year. Eventually, Clara grew out of it and everything was fine again.

Cut to fifth grade. My mom had just been diagnosed with breast cancer. She was literally diagnosed four days before the end of school so it didn't really affect me at school that year. The following year, however, was pretty hard for me. It was sixth grade and seeing my mom having all the surgeries and going through chemo was painfully hard for me. It's difficult to watch someone you love go through so much physical and emotional pain. By seventh grade, I had a better understanding of what was going on and it became harder to focus when I knew my mom was suffering. The way I dealt with it then was to just ignore it. Looking back, that wasn't the best way to handle that. However, I was a kid and I had never dealt with anything like that before. In my psychology classes in high school, I've learned about coping mechanisms and how some are healthier than others. Denial is one of the less effective coping mechanisms, because it means that you're simply ignoring a problem and burying the emotional pain deep inside and not properly dealing with it. This may help in the short term, but eventually all this emotional pain can boil over in some very difficult ways. Instead of dealing with the issue little by little, denial means that we end up having to deal with the emotional pain all at once denial is no longer an option.

Something that can be very helpful in dealing with difficult emotional issues is to see a therapist. I've never personally done this, but I know that it can be really beneficial. This can be helpful because it provides a forum to talk about feelings and experiences. One of the worst things to do during stressful times is to close off and isolate oneself. Sometimes people don't have someone with whom they can talk or perhaps they don't feel comfortable talking about it with a friend or family member because it's a sensitive issue. In those cases, a therapist can be someone who can listen and allow the person to talk about what's going on and perhaps offer some helpful advice if it's the right time for that. If you don't want to see a therapist, which is completely valid by the way, you may be able to confide in a trusted friend or adult – perhaps one of your parents, a relative, a teacher, or a family friend, as long as it's a trusted person who has your best interests at heart. What isn't helpful is to isolate and ignore your problems as that can actually make the situation worse. That is, unfortunately, what I did when my mom was diagnosed with cancer. I didn't know what to do with all my feelings so I stopped talking about it. In a sense, I pretended that it wasn't happening, but, of course, it was. Things didn't change for me until I was fortunate enough to find Camp Kesem, a camp for children affected by a parent's cancer. I was a camper at Camp Kesem for five years and now I'm a counsellor-in-training there.

The wonderful people at Camp Kesem helped me deal with my mom's cancer more than I can ever say. Camp Kesem is a national, free, sleepaway summer camp for kids affected by a parent's cancer and it is truly life-changing. Camp Kesem is the one place I can go where people instantly know what I'm going through because they've all been there themselves; the campers and the counsellors have all had similar experiences. Thus, they aren't freaked out or worse, feel sorry for me, because my mom had cancer. They understand who I am and what I've been through so I can just be a regular kid there.

I feel so blessed to have found Camp Kesem and I plan to eventually become a full counsellor there once I reach college. I've seen how much the counsellors have been able to help me because those counsellors have dealt with the same issues themselves. So now I hope to use the experiences I've had at Camp Kesem to give back to younger kids going through something similar to what I experienced. No child should feel the type of pain associated with having a parent with cancer, but these kids should at least have someone who understands them and can be there for them. In a sense, Camp Kesem is a type of group therapy where others listen and unconditionally support each other. There are many other organizations out there that offer similar types of support for kids going through other types of difficult situations. Whatever situation you encounter, try to find support either with a group or with a therapist. In my case, I've made amazing friends at Camp Kesem and this experience has helped shape me into the person I am today. If you haven't yet found your Camp Kesem, keep looking until you do. Your family can be helpful during stressful times, but sometimes we need to find someone or some group of people who will give us unconditional love and support during difficult times.

Things like this are very personal and solutions are always very individualized, so I cannot attempt to tell you what to do in every situation. What I can do is tell you is to never give up looking for help. No matter how bad things may look, there's always help out there so don't give up. Suicide is never an option. A lot of times, the media will unfortunately romanticize suicide, but remember that suicide is final. Suicide should never be considered no matter how bad life can get. If things feel that bad, you should immediately see a mental health professional. Suicide is a permanent solution to a temporary problem.

I have had my fair share of challenges, but what really shaped me was how I decided to cope with them. That's an important life lesson; our lives are determined less by what happens to us and more by how we deal with what happens to us.

Finding my supportive community at Camp Kesem truly helped me and I know there is help for you, no matter what the issue may be.

In addition to family issues, two issues that seem to affect the kids the most in my high school are anxiety and ADHD. I see these problems all the time with kids at school. These problems can be issues in and of themselves, and they also can lead to other issues such as depression if not adequately addressed. When kids are anxious all the time, they sometimes become very angry at others or at themselves and this can lead to depression. Because this type of problem can become worse if untreated, it is vital for such kids to get help by a licensed mental health professional. Same with ADHD which is a problem that causes difficulty with concentration, focus, and sometimes hyperactivity. ADHD can also be associated with anxiety and depression if not adequately treated. Sadly, many kids with these problems don't get adequate help and things can get worse over time resulting in problems at home and school. If you or someone you know is struggling with issues like this, try to help them find a licensed mental health professional.

When looking for a licensed mental health professional, try to find a counsellor or therapist who has experience with the specific issue and who seems to genuinely care about others. One on one counselling is usually the best way to start. Group counselling can also be helpful because it provides a chance to hear what others are going through and perhaps even help someone else going through a similar situation. If going to a mental health professional isn't a realistic option, perhaps your school or religious community has a counsellor who can help.

Conclusion

*W*ow, I'm impressed that you made it this far. Thank you so much for reading my book! I'm just a kid like you, just older, who has done her best to figure things out. I'm still figuring things out, but I've learned that life is about trying your best each and every day and doing a little better each day. I hope that I taught you something that will make your life a little better or a little easier. I just hope I didn't scare you too much for your first day of school. ☺

You may be absolutely terrified of high school from what you have seen in movies like "Mean Girls," "Clueless," and other movies. Although some of the stereotypes have some basis in reality, like the jocks being the most popular guys in school, some of them are so far from true; like that the cheerleaders are all stuck up jerks who hate each other. At least that's not true in my school.

Remember that school (and life) is what you make of it. You will meet people you don't like and you can simply ignore them. You will also meet some amazing people who can become life-long friends for you. Stick with those people. School itself isn't always going to be the most interesting thing in the world, but there are ways to make it better. Make sure you have a good group of friends and something you love doing outside of school.

If your first day of school is coming up, SLEEP. You will thank me later. Get your shit together and go to sleep. It's like when a bear is hibernating. They eat a ton of food so they don't have to later. If you sleep now, you won't have to get as much later. Well, maybe not but at least you're going to be a freshman so the workload won't be as bad as it will be when you are a junior or senior.

No matter what, never forget how important your friends and family are. They are your support system. Be there for them and let them be there for you.

Have fun! The next four years will go fast. You'll turn around and it will be time to go on to the next stage of your life so try to enjoy high school. One day you will look back on these days with nostalgia and wonder. Or not. ☺

I would like to conclude this book with an inspirational quote about high school: "High school is easy. It's like riding a bike, but the bike is on fire and the ground is on fire and everything's on fire because you're in hell," (Unknown).

Thank you for spending this time with me and I wish you all the best success and happiness in high school. Enjoy the ride!

Good luck!

~Ari

Acknowledgements

*T*hank you, Mom and Dad. Thank you so much for all of the support you have provided over the years. Whether it was Mom helping me stay up late to study for another test or Dad driving me to another soccer game, you are always there to offer me support. I will be forever grateful for everything you have done for me. I love you.

I also want to thank Camp Kesem for providing me with lasting and meaningful friendships that I will forever cherish. My Kesem friends have given me the best weeks and helped me through so many landmarks in my life.

Information About the Author

*A*rielle Morris is a senior at a high school just outside Los Angeles, CA. She is an AP Scholar with Distinction and anticipates earning her high school and International Baccalaureate Diplomas and the California State Seal of Biliteracy in 2020. In 2017, Arielle was selected for National Honor Society. She is the co-founder and President of her high school's French tutoring center. Arielle was an elite soccer player with the Real SoCal in the Developmental Player League, but put her playing career on hold after multiple concussions. Arielle is the oldest of four children, one of whom she likes occasionally.

Made in United States
North Haven, CT
18 June 2022

20385574R00093